THE TRUTH SHALL MAKE YOU FREE

THE TRUTH SHALL MAKE YOU FREE

by
David T. Demola

CHRISTIAN PUBLISHING SERVICES, INC
Tulsa, Oklahoma

Unless otherwise indicated, all Scripture quotations are taken from the *King James Version* of the Bible.

The Truth Shall Make You Free
ISBN 0-88144-092-2
Copyright © 1987
by David T. Demola
2177 Oak Tree Road
Edison, New Jersey 08820

Published by
Christian Publishing Services, Inc.
P. O. Box 55388
Tulsa, Oklahoma 74155

Printed in the United States of America
All rights reserved under International
Copyright Law. Contents and/or cover may
not be reproduced in whole or in part in any
form without the express written consent of
the Publisher.

CONTENTS

SALVATION	7
HEALING	11
THE BAPTISM OF THE HOLY SPIRIT	15
STUDY GUIDE	21

SALVATION

Welcome to the Family of God! The Bible states in Romans 10:9,10:

That if thou shalt confess with thy mouth the Lord Jesus, and shalt believe in thine heart that God hath raised him from the dead, thou shalt be saved.

For with the heart man believeth unto righteousness; and with the mouth confession is made unto salvation.

You have just made the greatest decision in your life. The Bible says that you have been called out of darkness into His glorious light (1 Peter 2:9). You have just changed citizenships and have become an ambassador for Jesus Christ and the Kingdom of Heaven (2 Corinthians 5:20).

The Truth Shall Make You Free

Although you may not feel any different, in actuality, your spirit has been made new (2 Corinthians 5:17). In fact, you have begun a life-changing experience that started when you were a sinner, and has transformed you into the righteousness of God in Christ Jesus (2 Corinthians 5:21). You have traded your ugly rags for the robe of righteousness that can only be put on at the new birth.

Remember, according to Ephesians 2:8,9:

For by grace are ye saved through faith; and that not of yourselves: it is the gift of God: Not of works, lest any man should boast.

It is nothing you have done, but because of the grace of God. He has called you and saved you from your own devices. In fact, it is because . . . **God so loved the world, that he gave his only begotten Son, that whosoever believeth in him should not perish, but have everlasting life** (John 3:16).

God's hand has been on you since you were in your mother's womb. Isaiah 44:24 says: **Thus saith the Lord, thy**

Salvation

redeemer, and he that formed thee from the womb . . . . His love is what drew you, although you really didn't realize your need for Him until now. Praise God.

Making the decision to accept Jesus as your personal Savior is just the beginning. To grow up in God, there are some steps you need to take. For instance, find yourself a Bible-believing church that can teach you the uncompromised Word of God. Also, study the Bible, not merely as a literary work, but as a book of instructions on how to live an overcoming life on this earth. The Bible states in Romans 12:1,2:

> **I beseech you therefore, brethren, by the mercies of God, that ye present your bodies a living sacrifice, holy, acceptable unto God, which is your reasonable service.**
>
> **And be not conformed to this world: but be ye transformed by the renewing of your mind, that ye may prove what is that good, and acceptable, and perfect, will of God.**

The Truth Shall Make You Free

Let your mind be washed clean by the Word of God (Ephesians 5:26). You see, as it says in Philippians 1:6, **Being confident of this very thing, that he which hath begun a good work in you will perform it until the day of Jesus Christ.** God will do for you what you could not do for yourself. He will make you a winner, an overcomer, the head not the tail and above not beneath. He will cause you to triumph in all things. He will prosper everything you put your hand to. (Refer to the following scriptures: 2 Corinthians 2:14, 1 John 5:4, and Deuteronomy 28:13.) He does all these things for you, not because of who you are, BUT BECAUSE OF WHOSE YOU ARE! Your salvation was paid for by the blood of Jesus when He died on the cross at Calvary (1 Corinthians 6:20). Jesus took our place at Calvary so that we might have eternal life. **For he hath made him to be sin for us, who knew no sin; that we might be made the righteousness of God in him,** according to 2 Corinthians 5:21.

HEALING

Your decision has opened up a wealth to you that no man can buy. You see, not only do you now have the blood of God flowing through your veins, and not only are you a joint heir with Jesus Christ with the promises made to Abraham back in Genesis 12:2,3, but you also have the gift of health in your mind, body and spirit.

The Bible states in 1 Peter 2:24...**By** (His) **stripes ye were healed.** You see, when Jesus died, He not only took our sins, He took our sickness too! (Isaiah 53:5.) Praise God!

Salvation has transformed your body into the temple of God, and, therefore, no sickness can dwell there. Throughout the scriptures, God makes reference to healing you. In James 5:14,15, the Bible states:

> Is any sick among you? let him call for the elders of the church; and let them pray over him, anointing him with oil in the name of the Lord:
>
> And the prayer of faith shall save the sick, and the Lord shall raise him up; and if he have committed sins, they shall be forgiven him.

Also, in Mark 16:18, **They shall take up serpents; and if they drink any deadly thing, it shall not hurt them; they shall lay hands on the sick, and they shall recover.** Even the Israelites, on their journey out of Egypt, never suffered colds, coughs, or the flu; as seen in Psalm 105:37: **He brought them forth also with silver and gold: and there was not one feeble person among their tribes.**

One of God's Hebrew names is Jehovah Rapha, which means *God the*

Healing

Healer. Why would God be referred to as the Healer if He didn't heal?

You need to set your mind, like a flint, on the Healer of your body, Jesus Christ. You need to study the Bible and learn of His healing power. In the Gospel of Matthew, chapter 4:23, it states, **. . . and healing all manner of sickness and all manner of disease among the people.** He has not changed His mind. He is still healing today, as seen in Hebrews 13:8: **Jesus Christ the same yesterday, and today, and for ever.** In Matthew 8:2,3, when the leper came to Jesus, saying: . . . **Lord, if thou wilt, thou canst make me clean,** Jesus put His hand out and said: **. . . I will; be thou clean.** At that very moment, his leprosy was cleansed!

That same healing power is yours today, JUST REACH OUT AND RECEIVE IT! Don't let others tell you God can't heal. Research for yourself, find out the truth. The Bible states in John 8:32, **And ye shall**

know the truth, and the truth shall make you free. My desire for you is that you begin to walk in that freedom so that you get hold of the power, the love and the gifts of God.

Sickness is a curse (Deuteronomy 28:15-68), and you have been redeemed from the curse of the law through your salvation. God does not use sickness, in any form, to teach His children a lesson. He does not need cancer to get man's attention. He sent the Holy Spirit.

THE BAPTISM OF THE HOLY SPIRIT

Another of God's wonderful gifts is the baptism of the Holy Spirit. God has manifested Himself in the Holy Spirit on this earth. The Holy Spirit is the Teacher, the Guide, the Paraclete, the Helper. He is the one who convicts man of his sin and shows man his need for God (John 14:26).

As Jesus stated in John 16:7-13 *(The Amplified Bible):*

> **However, I am telling you nothing but the truth when I say, it is profitable — good, expedient, advantageous — for you that I go away. Because if I do not go away, the Comforter (Counselor, Helper, Advocate, Intercessor, Strengthener,**

The Truth Shall Make You Free

Standby) will not come to you — into close fellowship with you. But if I go away, I will send Him to you — to be in close fellowship with you.

And when He comes, He will convict and convince the world and bring demonstration to it about sin and about righteousness — uprightness of heart and right standing with God — and about judgment.

About sin, because they do not believe on Me — trust in, rely on and adhere to Me.

About righteousness — uprightness of heart and right standing with God — because I go to My Father and you will see Me no longer.

About judgment, because the ruler (prince) of this world [Satan] is judged and condemned and sentence already is passed upon him.

The Baptism of the Holy Spirt

I have still many things to say to you, but you are not able to bare them nor to take them upon you nor to grasp them now.

But when He, the Spirit of Truth (the truth-giving Spirit) comes, He will guide you into all the truth — the whole, full truth. For He will not speak His own message — on His own authority — but He will tell whatever He hears [from the Father, He will give the message that has been given to Him] and He will announce and declare to you the things that are to come — that will happen in the future.

At your decision, the Holy Spirit comes to dwell within you and enables you, through His power, to continue the race. (Acts 1:8, **But ye shall receive power, after that the Holy Ghost is come upon you: and ye shall be witnesses unto me. . . .**)

Another purpose of the gift of the Holy Spirit is evidenced in Romans 8:26,27 (*The New King James Version*):

Likewise the Spirit also helps in our weaknesses. For we do not know what we should pray for as we ought, but the Spirit Himself makes intercession for us with groanings which cannot be uttered.

Now He who searches the hearts knows what the mind of the Spirit is, because He makes intercession for the saints according to the will of God.

Receiving of the gift of the Holy Spirit is evidenced by the speaking of tongues as seen in Acts 2:4, **And they were all filled with the Holy Ghost, and began to speak with other tongues, as the Spirit gave them utterance.** Also in Mark 16:17, **And these signs shall follow them that believe; In my name shall they cast out devils; they shall speak with new tongues.**

In order to receive this gift of the Holy Spirit, you need only ask, according

The Baptism of the Holy Spirt

to Luke 11:10-13 *(NKJ)*:

> For everyone who asks receives, and he who seeks finds, and to him who knocks it will be opened.
>
> "If a son asks for bread from any father among you, will he give him a stone" Or if he asks for a fish, will he give him a serpent instead of a fish?
>
> "Or if he asks for an egg, will he offer him a scorpion?
>
> "If you then, being evil, know how to give good gifts to your children, how much more will your heavenly Father give the Holy Spirit to those who ask Him!"

In the early church, one way the Baptism of the Holy Spirit, with evidence of speaking in tongues, was imparted, was by the laying on of hands (Acts 8:15-17 *(NKJ)*):

> who, when they had come down, prayed for them that they might receive the Holy Spirit.

The Truth Shall Make You Free

For as yet He had fallen upon none of them. They had only been baptized in the name of the Lord Jesus.

Then they laid hands on them, and they received the Holy Spirit.

All you need to do is ask the Father, right now as you are reading this book, and you can receive the baptism with evidence of speaking in tongues.

Glory to God, this gift is for everyone. A gift given by God can only be good, so receive it, gladly. Open your heart and mind to receive!

STUDY GUIDE

Below are a list of scriptures for your personal study in order to continue your growth in God's Word.

SALVATION

John 3:1-21; Romans 10:9,10; Ephesians 2:8,9; 2 Corinthians 5:17-21.

HEALING

Matthew 4:23,24; Hebrews 13:8; James 1:17; Deuteronomy 28:15-68; Isaiah 53:4,5; James 5:14,15.

BAPTISM OF THE HOLY SPIRIT

John 14:16,17,26; John 16:13; Acts 1:4,5,8; Galatians 3:14; Luke 11:10-13; Acts 2:4; Mark 16:17; Acts 10:44-46; Acts 1:8; Romans 8:26,27; 1 Corinthians 14:4; Jude 20.